apple

mela

pear

pera

orange

arancia

lemon

limone

grapes

uva

strawberry

fragola

watermelon

cocomero

coconut

cocco

banana

banana

raspberry

lampone

kiwi

kiwi

cherry

ciliegia

blueberry

mirtillo

plum

prugna

peach

pesca

fig

fico

pineapple

ananas

mango

mango

persimmon

cachi

cauliflower

cavolfiore

zucchini

zucchina

eggplant

melanzana

carrot

carota

potato

patata

cabbage

cavolo

tomato

pomodoro

spinach

spinacio

broccoli

broccolo

peas

piselli

pumpkin

zucca

butternut squash

zucca pepona

avocado

avocado

artichoke

carciofo

mushroom

fungo

radish

ravanello

garlic

aglio

onion

cipolla

beet

barbabietola

leek

porro

bell pepper

peperone

chili pepper

peperoncino

asparagus

asparago